Red Colt Canyon

Red Colt Canyon

Laurie Wagner Buyer

MUSIC MOUNTAIN PRESS
Westcliffe, Colorado

Red Colt Canyon

Copyright 1999 Laurie Wagner Buyer
Cover illustration © 1999 Larry Day
Design © 1999 Creativeminds.com

Published by
Music Mountain Press
Box 899 • Westcliffe, Colorado 81252
Voice and Fax: 719 783-9012
Email: mmp@creativeminds.com
Web site: http://www.creativeminds.com
ISBN: 0-9656126-8-6

Publisher's Cataloging-in-Publication
(Provided by Quality Books, Inc)

Buyer, Laurie Wagner, 1954-
    Red Colt Canyon : poetry / by Laurie Wagner
Buyer. -- 1st ed.
    p. cm.
    ISBN: 0-9656126-8-6

    1. West (U.S.)--Poetry.   I. Title.

PS3552.U8944R44 1999   811'.54
                        QBI99-561

For my mother
Joan
and in memory of my father
Frank Wagner
1931–1997

Heartwood

Unrumbled Thunder

Women of the Bridge

Heartwood

That First Summer

We lived in a 12 x 14 foot wall tent
slept on narrow single cots
ate our meals sitting on an igloo cooler,
the only flat, sturdy spot suited
to our rekindled hunger.

We listened to rain pound the nylon fly,
a pattering roar that warmed us to our
self-induced state of being drugged
by the earth beneath our feet, the light
bright and pearlescent in our eyes.

Every morning we set out fresh
to build a mile or so of barb wire
fence, four strand with treated posts.
The tractor noise and pounder wham
echoed in our ears for hours after.

Every afternoon, late, exhausted
by sun and wind and crazy thunder,
we sat in our pick-up cab living room
entertained by radio, books, and the most
recent mail from far away friends.

Nights redeemed our quest for quiet—
we held hands across the empty space
between our beds, the dog on a pallet
beside us, and listened to coyote questions,
owl answers, elk, night herons, the river.

We cooked out of cans and boxes, grew
grungy and tough, set out markers on
the land and on our hearts, never knowing
that nine years later we would still
be fixing broken dreams and busted wires.

Almost Anything

Standing at the window
you stare out at the storm
that's been brewing and
blowing since before dawn.

I watch your jaw tighten
and this hard silence
frightens me worse
than shouts or screams.

As you put on your down coat
and frayed wool cap
I go to get my boots
to help with night feeding.

You say, in a voice barely
a whisper, "You're not going,"
and you walk out wearily,
closing the door carefully.

Standing at the window
I listen to the bawling
cattle and watch wet
ragged calves drag by.

Sometimes I'd give
almost anything
if you would only just
break down, cuss, even cry.

Hot Iron

We mark our years together
by seasons, by each spring's
branding of another bunch
of high-tailed calves, the smoke
and smell of singed hair,
the air alive with expectation,
the searing sight of your blue
eyes tense under the tight brim
of a black, battered Stetson.

Brandings bind us better than gold rings,
shared names, a locked-box paper.
Once taken on the task becomes
reason for being, for fixing fence,
irrigating, cutting hay, feeding;
the gather and cut of our days,
the still stunning rebirth
of every entangled night.

Bawl and beller, kicks
and curses, bruises and burns,
the cussinest cattle chore
and the worst thirst ever born
of dust and wind and hope to hell
the weather holds. "Turn 'em out!"
I turn tired into your dirty arms,
a gritty kiss, the long, drinking,
sighing kind that brands us
with our common need.

Not Even Ashes

The fog frost is bitter
as biting as invisible insects
scavenging my face.

I am stripped bare
by your sacred silence
and the icy shoulder
you turn my way each day.

Yet, at night, our bodies
come clashing together
avenging archangels
full of fire and fury
using sex as swords
in an unwinnable war.

Then, by day's first light,
I am alone again
with no burnt offering
no smolder of a smile
not even ashes
to brighten your brow.

Suspended Animation

Anger's sour smell
hangs in the air between us
like the unwelcome whiff
of something going bad,
not yet rotten,
but turning, the core
growing soft and brown
while the flesh remains
uncommonly shiny, smooth,
full of color, calling:
touch, eat, swallow
the remembered sweetness.

We feel and fear the changing
center, shy from each other,
eyes wide, nostrils flaring
like horses spooked back
from a fetid winter kill;
a carcass only, but still some
tangible evidence to remind us
of what we once were.

The only hope to save what's left
is to freeze ourselves so solid
that we cannot open our mouths to speak,
cannot taste anything except ice.

Dancing In The Kitchen

After breakfast
while Vince Gill sings
"I Still Believe In You"
I dance in a small spot
between the sink and stove
my eyes closed
my arms holding air
until suddenly
you are there
clasping me close
leading our clumsy steps
giving us reason
to stay together
awhile longer.

Kneading Bread

Long before daylight, stove crackling,
coffee perking, I sprinkle yeast
on honeyed warm water, add salt
and oil, freshly ground whole wheat
flour which I stir and mix and fold
into fragrant bread dough.

I plunk it out onto an old
wood board while the wind woofs
hungrily at steam edged windows
and you toast your back
sip your morning cup and read about
falling cattle prices, costly feed.

In my worn sweats and slippers,
my hair twisted up in a slip-shod knot,
I labor the dough with supple floured
fingers, the fine rhythm of work—
push-pull-turn, push-pull-turn,
transfiguring sticky wet into
elastic glossy smooth.

I feel your arms ease around me from
behind, your chest flannel full
against my curved back, your mouth
moist and breathy on my ear
moving wisps of escaped hair
tickling and teasing along my neck
sending spine shivers quivering to my toes.

Closing my eyes to this bliss kiss
kindness, your warmth weakens me,
melts me into an embrace that turns
me from the swollen dough to place
white hands upon your tan face,
leaves me wondering what it is
about kneading bread
that makes you need me.

Present In Darkness

Present in darkness before dawn,
the appearance of a hundred head of elk
chained out across wind swept meadows.

Reforged in that moment alone with you
on the back stoop, the flux of memory:
elk spilling off aspen choked ridges

to engulf the feed sled loaded heavy
with baled hay, the molten weight
of our first stolen kisses.

Past and present link us, weld our
want for permanence in a world that
daily disappears before our tired eyes.

We are cold. There is work to be done.
Still we stand, shoulder to shoulder, until
the last shadowed shapes fade from sight.

Walking the Redmon Ditch

On the old Mikel's place,
Mertensia, tall chiming bells,
nod in a mid-morning breeze
and the aspens quiver overhead
matching the shiver your touch
brings, the wild ripeness
of a long awaited summer.

Cutting sods with perfect precision
you make magic with wayward water
sending a silver spill over
the bank edge to moisten meadows
where Pedicularis and Gentian part
a growing green gown with purple.

You shoulder your mud caked shovel,
hold my dirty hand with the loose,
long time stance of a lover whose
fingers fit mine like puzzle pieces
crafted of bone and darkened skin.

Sun and shadow flicker
playfully over your closed eyes,
your open, waiting face.

The sky spins.
The earth's energy enters us.

What leaves, flying free, is as proud
and predatory as the hovering hawk,
as light and airy as a champagne
butterfly dancing by.

The Truth About Toilets

The truth about toilets
is that they take tending
like livestock in winter
who demand feeding
and a garden in summer
that wants weeding
or a lover whenever
the longing for touch
overtakes every other need.

So humble on my knees,
the scrub brush, sponge
and astringent cleanser
clean much more than just
the porcelain bowl.

The whirl of water sucks away
not only dirt and waste
but the bitter taste
of argument and anger
when I should have forgiven
every little oversight and sin
forgotten the tangle of everyday
tasks and made love to you
right then and there
on the cool tile floor.

Praying For Rain

On the day of the first summer storm
I turn easily into your arms
as open and anxious as dry earth
waiting for the wet of lips and kiss.

I soak up your strength and scent,
swell with self satisfaction
sparkle like sun spots glinting
off the watery afternoon light.

Quiet and serene, you sit on the edge
of the bed to pull on dusty boots.
I lay spread over the colorful quilt
like butter melting on oven warm bread.

I sip your shy smile, drink in
the dripping eaves and cloud damp sky,
swallow the sweet sensation
of supplication and answered prayer.

The Last Good Days

The last good days of summer were gone.

Old Jack's eye bulged and broke
ran his blindness out
onto the damp ground
in the shelter of willows
where he wandered lost,
whinnying alone—

then you were gone with the gun
to say good-bye
but I had no tears
to cry, empty and dry,
like the great grasses
that marked this year
as the decade's best.

Left behind in the house
I turned on lights in every room
to melt away the darkness
where you walked,
to strengthen your aim;
and I hugged myself
in the autumn silence
listening for the sound
of just one shot.

Waiting by the back door
the dog lay quiet, his head on his paws,
his eyes wide and watching.

Headlights waved beams of brightness
as the backhoe belched sooty smoke
and ripped through weeds and rocks
to expose an open mouth of earth
wide enough to swallow
a huge black draft horse,
giving him some honor
other than coyotes and ravens.

When you returned, your jaw
clenched against sympathy,
I simply took the rifle
and put it away.

Cowboy Nursing

The hot flash shiver chills of flu
overtake me past midnight and
I ache like a roadkill rabbit
before it dies. Moonlight,
painful as snow blindness,
stings my eyes where I watch
the night wind whip grass seed heads
against the frosted windowpane.

You don't know much
about nursing
except for poking pills
down the cold throats
of scour sick calves
or stitching up a prolapsed cow.
You'd never think to boil up
a cup of tea, wring out wet rags,
or rub my muscle sprung back.

Yet, instinct, born of the war
and many long nights alone,
wakes you in the deep silence.
You pull me, fetal curved,
into the womb of your own fierce heat,
tuck my rump into the v-notch
of your groin and wrap an iron arm
under the soft swell of my sweaty breasts.

You sleep again and I match
your even heartbeat breathing
until the night grows gray
with newborn morning light.

Christmas Dawn

Slipping from bed to start fires
you leave a warm hollow place
which I curl myself into, settling
in the leftover heat of your space.

Such a sigh of pure, light contentment
triggered by this small little niche
because you have left in your absence
a gift so abundant, so rich.

The feeling lasts but a moment
until your essence, inhaled, is all gone
nothing compares to the scent of your hair
on your pillow in a cold Christmas dawn.

White Noise

Night sounds pulse through an open window
screening the city onto my bare skin

before they are sucked and blown
by the buzz of an oscillating fan.

Any suggestion of sleep eludes me,
escapes into the flip of a digital clock.

I sweat onto fine paisley sheets and miss you
breathing the best of your dreams beside me.

Restless, surrounded by strangers
and the white noise of nothingness,

I ache for the annoyance of mice
scurrying along log walls,

the balm of a blanket woven out of
wished-on and fallen shooting stars.

Where the Road's Going

Where the road cuts a straightened swath
through stunted pine and sage
it realigns our separate lonelinesses
into one long reaching ribbon toward home.

Not yet sixty-seven, my father's gone one month past.
Your mother, a decade short of a century,
holds her life stretched thin in a search
for air at the end of an oxygen line.

Our granddaughter toddles with cow dogs,
scoops dry desert dirt in her tiny hands.
Our grandson, in the chute, kicks and clambers,
ready to be born, a bronc rider already like his father.

Caution: Elk Crossing.
Conejos River Overflow.
The Oldest Church in Colorado.
Bulls 4 Sale.

Antonito. La Jara,
where a neat white house with lacy blue trim
faces the highway head on and the Sangres,
emboldened with old snow, come closer and closer.

Red Colt Canyon

Galloping uphill toward
my half-wakened vision,
the pounding sound
of *Red Colt Canyon*
runs from a highway sign
in southeastern New Mexico
spurring in me such a rush
of loosened desire
I panic, searching
the landscape for memory
or the fleet foreshadowing
of an encounter yet to come.

Riding the crest of the cedared
ridge, breath held, my hands
reach for the receding dash,
you brake sharply
for a tight turn,
point and cry out:
"Look! Road Runner!"

Plumed, spotted, the long-legged bird
races the edge of the asphalt
then escapes into rocks and brush.

Around the end of the bend,
flattened beside a melting bank
of the New Year's first snow,
his mate lies, still bright, burnished
by an awkward slant of sun.

Whatever warning this is,
everything in me cools:
I hear the strange colt snort
behind my shaking shoulder,
taste a tangle of despair
as I swallow tightly
the tough bit of a fading day.

Chiseled In Stone

Ranching's teaching me to let my
husband be what he was born to be,
cut from the earth, warped by wind,
each day the work grinding him away,
shaping him, making him into an old man
who wants no other realm than this hunk of dirt:
the dust, small animals flushed from the grass,
as the tractor makes endless rounds with birds
circling in the open sky, a rain storm coming,
and all the time in the world for him to think
about living a tightrope life so close to death.
The land carves a poetic code on his face,
scribes it with an unwritten language
I am always trying to decipher.

Until I Run Out of Thread

Like an old coat
I've outgrown you
stretched in a different direction
until the seams of our marriage
pull tight, near to splitting,
and the sleeves of our loving
are too short, leaving me
exposed and cold, unprotected.

Yet I smile putting you on
letting your latent warmth
settle across my shoulders,
letting your rich earthy smell
take me back to the days
when we fit together like hands
clasped in perfect sized gloves.

New coats cram the front
of my heart's closet
but still I reach far
to the back for you—
my favorite, my most
comfortable companion.

I stitch your raveling hem
mend your torn cuffs
patch your worn collar;
I will labor to keep you
whole and close
until I run out of thread.

Heartwood

Ringed close and tight
your years create
such a solid core
hard, durable
so substantial
I grow from you
soft, light alburnum
and your strength
sings in my veins
sap rising to fill my need.

Younger, easily scarred
I seek seasoned shade
hold tight to your lee side
out of the drying wind
press my face to rough
bark knowing your center
shelters and saves.

Someday the lightning
strike of age will crack
us apart, inevitable
separation, but your
spirit will stand
full of pitch and fire
long after dead branches
grace the barren ground.

Unrumbled Thunder

She Waits

The land was never ours
for all our wanting.

We came, desired, took.

We never asked.

Like a woman taken and left,
she remains silent and scarred,
alone in an aloneness
we cannot feel.

Beneath her aged and wrinkled face
a child's complexion hides
behind a flare of skirt and apron
where we never looked.

Undiscovered now,
as ever,
she waits.

Killdeer's Cry

Her staccato voice pierces the morning
draws me away from the earth,
the tang of sage, the perfume of pine,
to her darting dance of white wings
flashing against the azure sky.

She catches me unaware:
this killdeer, then pining snipe,
a pair of mated geese swing low
and drop to strut the pasture knoll
with bracing honks and sighs.

So much has died and gone—
so much remains beyond
the snow's last pale shadow
where my boots sink in mud
forgiving the frost filled ground.

And with this melting, an ease
inside of me, a giving up,
a letting go, the startled surprise
of my own off key wailing
whipped away by warmer wind.

Seduction

It surprised me when the sun,
coming out slowly from behind
weeks of wintry clouds,
touched my face with such warmth
I felt I was being admired
by the weary eyes
of a thousand bloodied warriors

and the world went to its knees
before my enraptured face
and my trembling hand reached out
to touch the harsh bark of a bare
aspen tree, steadying myself,
my legs weak with longing
and love of the very air.

I hesitated only a moment,
then closed my eyes and sank
to the wet waiting ground
where last year's leaves clung
to me like kisses, sun dogs
danced on my inner lids and
I opened myself
to the seduction of a snipe's
wind-rushed-in-wings song.

Buried Angels

Even in early June
frost covets each night
drought hangs heavy
seven weeks since snow
and counting clouds for rain.

Still, paintbrush poke red heads
through crack-patterned soil
grass turns tough
on slender stems
tasting the constant wind.

Walking saves nothing
but puffs of chalk white dust
rise around my ankles
like the dry buried breath
of long lost angels.

Letting Loose My Hair

Walking into coming night,
the virgin air rinsed by rain and
expectant with unrumbled thunder,
I let loose my hair for
the wind to finger at will
while my senses swell,
full as the banked power
of the brimming river.

The wonder of it returns
in darkness captured
between lightning flashes,
before bed, bent like a bow,
brushing my charged hair,
I spark with the electric arc
of the summer storm.

Such Small Elegance

A cottontail sits frozen
in a shaft of sunlight,
ears stiff as pricks of silence,
a twist of half eaten clover
clenched in her teeth.

Such small elegance graces my
morning, reminds me to be still,
tells to wait and watch, to let life
pass me by once in awhile.

The sun shifts under a cloud
and the cottontail disappears
in gray-patterned pine shade.

Clarity comes quickly,
creature born, quietly delivered,
leaving me wiser in ways to hide.

—for my mother

Georgia O'Keefe Paints

Georgia O'Keefe paints
late morning's face
with clouds
gunmetal gray
over layers of baby blue
and virgin white
a violent softness in the sky
that highlights the bones beneath:
dark eyebrow of the ridge
an aqualine nose of trees
curved ear of the river
broad grassy cheeks
sharp jawline of lichened rock
the open mouth of my adoration.

Releasing the Browns

Whatever wonder born of watery birth
stays hidden in the trouts' gills and fins,
a mystery to me, earth walker, lover
of warm blooded mammals and birds.
I have never been drawn to fish
until now, seeing them slip like
dark dreams from bucket to stream.

Pond reared innocents released in wild water,
they have so much to learn as I watch
them disappear in muddy swirls from
sun-sheened shallows into willow
shadowed pools. I say not good-bye,
but lie low, beware the diving osprey,
the heron, and artfully crafted false fly.

Partnered now, wind and rain play
new tunes to this old folk dance:
elusive brown, study in liquid grace,
leaps and flees, I pursue, clumsy in
my boots, arm outstretched to clinch
the perfect cast, realizing joy comes
not from holding on but in letting go.

—for Bill and Jo Murray

Romancing the River

Until I have felt underfoot her every curve and bend
and heard the sound of her rippled voice
changing from chute to riffle to pool where willows
drape reflections of her thousand faces,
how can I say I know her?

Until I have whispered to her in wonder, stretched
out open on her soft and grassy sides or reached shyly
into the unknown clefts of her undercut banks
and delved the old mysteries of her wild running,
how can I say I want her?

Until I have met and mastered the minds
of other worshippers—occult osprey, reclusive brown,
flash fire of leaping rainbow and hidden heron who
rises from the water phoenix-like, a cloud of mystic smoke—
how can I say I accept her?

Until I have walked alongside her in every waking
hour, dawn through dusk, and longer still, night into day,
and seen her dark flanks caressed by sun, silvered with
starlight and drank mesmerized from her secret springs,
how can I say I understand her?

Until I have held the haunting silence of her winter
heart in my shaking hands, counted the quick pulsed
flood of spring awakening, yearned for the ripe beauty
of her summer dress and coveted her autumn glory,
how can I say I possess her?

An hour or two is never enough. Even offering
one day diminishes the devotion she so deserves.
Until I plunge into giving everything, vulnerable,
as naked and unashamed as her own soul,
how can I say I love her?

These Things of the Earth

Lake mirrored cloud free sky, trout rise;
willow shade caressing lavender flags,
a swallow's swoop to mud-dabbed nest.

Slapping wind full of spilled thunder,
midnight lightning startling the dark,
a moth battling the rain-specked window pane.

River voice chanting below flooded banks,
dawn light painting the water bronze and gold,
a cottontail scratching her ear in dewy grass.

These simple, ordinary, everyday,
miraculous things of the earth.

—for Jo on her
76th birthday

Bareback

Seeping through dusty jeans
his heat thaws my thighs
loosens chilled stiffness from my spine

and my shoulders relax, breasts bounce,
clench muscles grip his heaving sides
as we lope circles in dusky sage.

Hoof beats pound through my pelvis
uniting hips and hocks—
his heart throbs with mine

as we shift our center of balance
switch leads on the fly,
nostrils flared, sweating,

we cut the last of the day
from October's long-edged night.

Some Somnolent Power

While I turned back swathe bales, an owl whispered
from ditch willows, her head cocked curiously,
her eyes slit shut against sharp September sun.

I imagined her abrupt awakening in the deep shade
where she rested, hiding out the day,
waiting for night's cool air to caress her wide wings.

In mid-flight she floated like a scrap of fog, gray
mist against mature green, a drift of thistle down,
an eye blink of a dream, then suddenly she was gone.

Thunder rumbled in her wake as if some great
somnolent power, disturbed, rolled over once,
then settled back to sleep.

I whistled softly to the dog, walked slow
and silent through fresh cut stubble,
handled each bale like new blown glass.

Little Live Things

Redder than the rich earth
that grew them round and firm
beets bleed into my hands,
little live things turned
hot and slick from the scald
of boiling water, icy
from the rinse of October river.

Methodically, I slice off
stalked wilted heads
strip burgundy skins
cut fine-haired reaching roots.

I dice them into steaming vinegar
mix in sugar, turmeric, mustard seed.
I pickle, pack and can, and leave
them gracing the cellar shelves
like preserved Christmas decorations.

For days after the sacrifice
my hands stay stained
with the gift they gave.

Gooseberries

My old sorrel is staid;
he stands content in the shade
of a homestead shed on a bright
August afternoon while I sweat
hurriedly picking ripe berries.

Holding each cane high,
exposing wicked hooked thorns,
I reach anxiously for globlets
grown purple-rich with bitter
juice, whining with guardian wasps.

I am clothed ankle to wrist to escape
ants and insects and a floppy brimmed
hat protects my exposed face,
hovers over my head
like a melting, misplaced halo.

In this seemingly benevolent battle,
summer's last reaching leap for life,
I am bewitched by the transformation
of peel and pulp into wine colored jelly,
tart with the taste of turning leaves.

Late, long after the sun's half closed eye
winks behind the peaks, I lie awake,
my hands fiery with need, still picking,
every razored scratch ablaze, every thorn
tip working its way toward my too soft heart.

A Drumming of Distant Hooves

Thin as a much sharpened sickle, a slice
of moon scoops out a bite of indigo sky
and reflects yesterday's lost light on this day.

The air, new, neutral, not yet warmed with sage
and sweat, the unwieldly scent of thistle or over
ripe wild rose, belongs yet to the unknown night.

Left over in the mud from a late unexpected rain
a buck's signature track walked the wire fence
seeking an easy leap downhill to brush cover.

Backed up against the blown wall of another
storm front, a bank of barely gilded clouds
gathers like the rush and shush of sea foam

and a drumming of distant hooves calls
out the changing hour while I stand high
above the cutbank watching, waiting:

mammoth, wolves running elk, buffalo,
warring Utes, or just the return of thirsty
draft mares from the willow-hidden river.

October Evening

Up the ridge, into the sun,
scrambling on thin shale, I coach
myself: don't run, stop, sit,
breath, slow, slower, think…

The cow elk's trail is long since
lost in a welter of tracks woven
through new mud and fading snow
patches shadowed by black timber.

Shaggy manes push their knobby
heads, the color of bleached bones,
up through decomposed granite, red
now in the light like old dried blood.

Coyote scat, curled thick with twisted
rodent hair, lies gray and rotting
next to a track imprinted with the echo
of a long, thin wail sounded far north.

Bear mauled, shattered, the stump
where I sit feels as ancient as the earth,
venerable, its weathered roots reaching
deep into pine needle loam.

A thin trickle of sweat crawls
slowly down my spine; I walk again,
into the sun, into the setting sun,
into the white light chill of the sun.

Nighthawks and Owls

White barred wings
dive deep in the dawn sky
guide me on a dark trail
with nighthawk shrieks
and the booming roar
of feathered autumn air.

This trio has traced
my path every day
leading me up the ridge
woven with sage and
spruce, the sweet smell
of gone-gold aspen and pine.

Hawking forth casual
conversation, two owls
call from spired spots
high up against
the brightening skyline
forecasting frozen nights.

An aberrant wind keens
crazily from the east
stirs drought dried grasses
into an autumn dance
of death, spilling seeds
in a rustling shiver of sound.

It is here in this high place
that the old souls speak
nighthawks and owls answer
I listen, listen carefully
and learn, letting the wind
scour clean my young skin.

Naked in Starlight

Outside the long, low kitchen window
winter wind whips last fall's tall grasses
and they are running, running hard,
heads bent, but they go nowhere,
they stay fixed, rooted in homesteader's sod
while I rush around in my frantic daily race.

Without roots I bounce off the walls,
denting the hard, smoke stained logs
set so surely, so deliberately a century ago.
I have nothing to cling to, no hold to stay;
the voice of the wind laughs, taunts,
tells me I am nothing but tumbleweed.

The early comers built thick and solid,
rebuffed the wind with windows near the ground
so they could see the grass, the hops vines,
the rhubarb, the tansy, all tap rooted,
set forever, reaching as deep as the river rock
so even their spirits stayed.

Not graced with fragile flower or even leaf,
I am nipped and pruned and wind shaped
into something shocked and stunted.
I have no seed, no spore, no tough tendril
stretching out to anchor me, to establish
my living in just one time and place.

My future blooms before me like a sepia dream:
withered, I roll and roll out of control
toward some empty horizon,
until, snagged in sagging rusted wire, I hang,
a sorry skeleton, but, oh, how stunning
I'll look naked in starlight.

Coming in Out of the Cold

Coming in out of the cold
wood stove warmth steals
my last pulse of strength
and I slip into a chair, ebbing,
like my hat's ice shrinking in the sink.

Serene under a fine sift of snow,
the world returned to winter
while I slept restless, dreaming
those sullen, stubborn dreams
I swore I'd never dream again.

But the mares' broad backs
were laced like snowy bridal gowns
and their tug chains jingled
merry as the cow herd trailed in
for the treasure of hay I fed.

Blankets of cloud cover cuddled
the wan eastern disk of gold light
and dim sun dogs danced
north and south of its guiding
center as I walked slowly west

for no real reason except my numb feet
searching for secrets hidden
beneath the crust and fluff,
for the faintest awakening
of the still, silent, dreamless land.

Horse Barn on a Winter Day

Wind worn, rain stained, much more
than weathered wood, the barn
breathes an air of old content
as settled as its sill logs sunk
deep in this rocky river bottom soil.

Every callused hand that ever lifted
the forged iron door latch remains,
imprinted with aged gray grain;
children's cries, laughter, sun beam
spirits window dance and at night
a ghostly wheezed breeze crawls
bright through moonlit cracks.

All the women who ever loved
in this rough plank loft stayed,
their sweet smell edged with the fragrance
of new made hay, the sharp clawed
tang of cat marked territory.

How still the old harness hangs on hand
carved pegs, shadowed with the song
of hoof stomp and tug chain ching.
Sun baked, the tin roof's rusted as dark
as the dried blood of butchered beeves.

Early Winter Walk

Through a blue white world I walk
this early winter evening,
the snow insulates out everything
beyond the bridge, the far ridge,
the line of pine leaning south
so that stillness itself is sound
against falling flakes on my face.

A woman could wait a lifetime
for this kind of beatitude:
tiptoe, sinking my tongue into
a snowy mound atop a fence post,
my hands grip white wires
and stretch into ecstasy.

Women
of the Bridge

Women of the Bridge

—a found poem inspired by Kathryn Eastburn's
review of Ramona S. Diaz's film "Spirit
Rising" in the Rocky Mountain Women's
Film Festival Guide, October 1997.

Before Conquistadors and
the heavy cloak of Catholicism,
Filipino women freely celebrated
a rich history of equality and self-rule.

They honored the tradition of
having only one child
and believed that every woman
crossed the black river of death
with the help of a man who loved her.

To prepare for their ultimate passing,
ancient island women
took many lovers in a lifetime,
searching for just the right man
to accompany them on their last journey.

Now, only leather-faced, toothless
women in white lace veils
remember the incredible legend
of the women of the bridge.

The mythological story stirs the edges
of my consciousness and I watch men
with barbaric, primitive awareness,
wondering how many lovers lie between
my beating heart and the dark water.

Grave Robbers

They found her in a small cave
On Big Twin Creek
Wrapped in decayed beaded buckskin
With two hundred elk teeth around her neck
And horse hair dangles tangled
In her long dark hair
One hundred and fifty years
Lying in peace
With only pine shadow
And the rushing song of the creek.
But they pulled her into the light
Disjointing spirit and bones
Dismantling what was a sacred place
To take her away to Laramie
In the back of a rattling truck
To study and pry and pretend
They need to know more about her.
Five hundred miles south of the sacrilege
Just hearing her story
I could have told them what they need to know
That in that lost and lonely place
Where I used to walk and ride
Where boulders, water, moss and sky
Kept watch for countless nights
In that place now torn and ruined
I hear her cry.

—for a fourteen year old
Gros Ventre girl

Abandoned Sheep Wagon
at Four Horse

A hole in summer-darkened clouds
filtered sunset through storm
where a woman walked after the rain
through the wreckage of a camp
at the old ghost station.

Broken wheels, rusted hubs,
bullet-racked wash tub and
a shattered pitcher; a scrap
of dirty canvas, some nails amid
the weathered boards and a button.

The wind blew a ragged wail
whipping long unbound hazel hair
across her aged olive eyes
and when she could see again
she spotted a piece of half
buried crockery caught in
the ruin of things forgotten.

She dug cautiously with
a small, dull pocket knife,
dumped out the damp dirt and
polished the ivory cup clean
with the hem of her flannel shirt.

Standing still in the day's last light
she could see a sagebrush fire
burning bright
smell coffee and biscuits
hear a baby cry
and far off over the ridge
the bleat of many sheep
being brought home
through a dim hole in the night.

—for Faye Lavengood

There Were No Women

Mail came up but twice a week
when the dirt road could stay open
no telephone to salve the stretch
of endless days with a silent man,
the nearest neighbor miles away
and there just were no women.

Morning and evening chores to do,
planting and gardening in spring,
harvest and canning in the fall,
no helping hands to ease the load,
no laughing smiles or teasing fights
because there were no women.

In memory my mother's face or
those of sisters, aunts, and friends,
in magazines those feminine dreams
of playing house and beauty shop
turned so lost and left behind
because there were no women.

So I sang to goats, hugged the cats,
conversed with the sad-eyed dog,
whispered words to shaggy horses,
held close a pine tree's roughened bark,
wept silly tears, hurt and harsh,
because there were no women.

Children came, barely conceived,
and cursed before believed in,
dark red rushes slipping away
in wadded sheets and bloodied fear
left me shivering to wash alone
because there were no women.

I was more tired than lonely, more
lonely than afraid, my heart turned hard,
my hands grew raw, my soul dried
and shriveled—near to dying, way past
crying because in all those long gone years
there just never were any women.

Letters

All her life she lived remote on ranches,
far from folks and goings on
harboring small happinesses in her heart
but she had her letters and she wrote at dawn
when the fires had been built and the coffee pot perked.

On snowy evenings with the day's long list of chores done
she curled by the wood stove pen and pad in hand
the kerosene lamp glow haloing her blithe face
while her husband shook his head, sighing,
and turned back to his newspaper.

Every mail day was Christmastime,
every opened envelope a gift;
for in the ink she saw eyes and
in the feel of the paper she felt hands
and in written words she heard voices, laughter, songs.

Even after the road pushed through,
with easy access to town and the treat of people,
she wrote to far away family and friends,
she wrote to strangers who knew more about her life
and her love of the land than anyone.

She saved her legacy of letters,
lining them in boxes by name and date.
They became her reason for being,
the only thing she had to call her own
and in the end it was enough.

—for Virginia Bennett's
ranch wife in her
poem "Tapestry of Knots"

Ghazel Written on the Road to Guffey

Stonecrop and cancerroot thrive on a rocky trail.
Some things grow well on such small sustenance.

Garo flat is a painter's palette of gray sage and white loco
dabbed with scarlet paintbrush and purple penstemon.

Three buck antelope bound from sun-warmed beds
to stand stiff-legged, silouhetted against a basalt background.

The old highway undulates, a worn windblown ribbon
embraced on both sides by gnarled pine and bunch grass.

Afoot in a fence corner, two ranchers work cattle with canes.
With hobbled gaits and outstretched arms, they dance.

Wolves pace the perimeter of a chain link environment.
Eyes, fire bright, see beyond the hold of their human pack.

In the greenhouse the air is heavy and heady with promise.
A little soil and water, the sun, dirty hands, health, and healing.

— for Chris Rivers

From The Edge

From the edge
of the wrinkled bed
eye level with the earth
mountains lift
against a moon set sky
like quizzical eyebrows
questioning my step
through the window
onto alpine tundra.

Myriad twists and turns
brought me to this long
straight view
foreshortened by angle
and incredible light
until the horizon's
within reach of
my awakening hand.

If not for my lover's arm
encircling my waist
and a barrier of glass
I'd be above timberline
my face submerged
in a snow melt pool
until I emerged
antlered and elusive
as an autumn elk.

Diana

When I walked from
the shadow of willows
she stood alone
bathed in fresh light
gracing the river's edge.

Her fly rod, held aloft,
caught the sun and flashed
like lightning flung from her hand.
Shimmers danced in the dark curls
above her high brow and reflected
back diamonds hung in her ears.

Everything—
even the rush of the river—
stopped.

A redtail screamed.

Horses broke from the brush,
shattering the spell
like a struck mirror.

The roar of the water
returned, filling
my eyes as I walked,
casting the current onward.

—for Diana Doyle

Lady of the Night

Some come to me awkward
and uncertain, too young
to be called men, too anxious
to yet be boys, so I wrap
them in smiles and easy
laughter, untie their tongues
and teach them the art
of talk and touch.

Some I spot as soon as they
crawl in the door, their eyes
small and hard. They are quick
and cruel and I know at home
they beat their wives so I close
my eyes and shut my soul against
their emptiness and fear.

Some I wait for, like those
who handle horses, their eyes
so open I see landscapes,
places I've never been except
in dreams; their hands, callused
and slow, soothe my quivering
flesh, move like magic until
my nostrils flare and I rear
to meet sound and smell, earth
and air. They stay on my tongue,
echo in my ears for days after.

On Sundays I do not work
but walk alone along the river
where my gods live, the holy
rush of water below the willows
haunts me every night until
I can return, leave my clothes
on the grassy bank and slip
like an otter through deep pools,
the liquid like dark silk
on my fine tuned skin.

—for Laurina

She Loved Horses

She loved horses
the way she loved men
the way they smelled
the way they moved
the way they felt under her hand.

It was something in the way
they feared being
caught and tied
but came to her anyway
and gave into their need
to be cared for
for tenderness
for affection.

She loved the good in them
as well as the bad
accepted their antics
and occasional ornery streaks
as part and parcel
of the reward she felt
when she moved with them
that flow of freedom
she found no where else.

Most of all she loved
the power of persuasion
alive in her hands
her voice
the way she could coax
them to her will
make them go anywhere
do anything
as long as she honored
with kindness
the awkwardness of
their developing hearts.

—for Sandy Champion

Wooing the Wanton Mare

After so many years afoot
I felt the mare would be mine:
hauled home in the back
of an old stock truck
she stood trembling at the far end
of the chewed pole corral, black
as a burnished raven's wing.

Oh! The names he called her flew
from his mouth like hot spit,
while she whirled and ran dust clouds,
tucked her head tight in a corner
and kicked, righteously, heels high,
until, he left in disgust, flinging the halter
down in the powder fine manure dirt.

When he was gone I stole down
to see her, sat on the top pole
and talked her pinned ears up, her
nostrils open, so fluttery they moved
like moths against the night of her nose,
until at last she came to me on her own,
her deep eyes wide with the weight
of danger, her dark face softened
by a little crooked star.

Once saddled she rode like a willow
bending in the breeze, pliant, at ease,
everything in her alert, anxious,
as giving and willing as a ready woman.
That she would come to me but never to him
rubbed us as raw as a gall, irritating our flesh
like an unanswerable ache.

Everything broke loose with my going:
my greatest regret after so many years
of giving in was leaving the mare,
her fine head hung over the gate
watching me drive away in the rain.

—for Sis

Equine Chatter

I.

I miss horses more than
I can say and my life seems
empty without them, but
that's how it is when you
live in the middle of
San Antonio. When I
was twenty or so I worked
on my Aunt and Uncle's
dude ranch, the Elkhorn,
in Estes Park and knew more
than 30 horses by name and
put in 12 hour days packing and
guiding, breakfast and supper rides.
I remember all those horses
with affection and exasperation—
the ones that wouldn't tie and
the ones that would lay down and
roll in the creek with a dude
on their backs. We had a big
brass-colored gelding called Lucky
that would lean back on his halter rope
in his stall and go to sleep until he was
startled then he would fall down
with a terrible crash. I could have
done it forever but decided to get
through University instead.
Another good wrangler
gone to hell.

II.

I am no longer afoot.
I can't afford a horse but
secured a position as riding instructor
at Fort Sam Houston stables.
I'll help teach short people how
to saddle and unsaddle and
ride without reins.

There's this lovely gelding,
four years old, going sour,
a slight little thing, maybe 15 hands,
in a stall all the time,
getting wilder and wilder,
can't put anybody on him,
nobody has time to work him,
so I guess I will; he's very
affectionate, but when he gets
out of that stall, he just
wants to run and buck and
shoot the moon. If I don't work him
he'll end up sold to a killer.
He has a splendid head and
is nicely put together, slim legs,
small feet, dark bay with just
a touch of white on the hinds.
I solved the mystery of where
he came from, the VT ranch
across the border. Like all Mexican
ranch horses he has that well-formed
conformation, beautiful head,
good legs and feet but narrow,
no chest at all but lots of bottom.
Tomorrow I will longe my Mexican
ranch horse, let him tear up jack
in the round pen. Maybe I
can make something of him.

III.

Another bit of luck,
a full-time Army sergeant,
a Buffalo Soldier re-enactor,
keeps his mare at the stable
and if I split the feed bill
he says I can ride her.
She's a great tall railroad bridge
of a horse, a thoroughbred off the track,
she never knows where all her legs are
at any given time and turns like a train,
just one big joint after another
coming around the bend,
but a horse is a horse
at this stage of my life
and being busy with animals
means I'm as busy as a windmill:
I guess life will make
something of me after all.

—for Paulette Jiles, in her own words

Grandmother's Bowl

Clutched between bent arm and breast,
my grandmother's bowl warms to beaten
butter, embraces the eggs, yields
to the thick mix of sugar, flour, salt,
runs with the tang of lemon and fine
grated peel, gives up her gift of batter
to a waiting greased pan then sits
soiled but beautiful beside the sink.

As the kitchen fills with fragrant
baking cake, I take her in hand,
rinse her clean, slowly immerse gray
crockery side, carefully scrub
inside out with a worn green sponge,
rinse again in lukewarm water
then dry, the white flour sack
towel hugging her curves tight.

—for my father's mother,
Olive Jane

Black Lace

Petticoats and panties,
hose strung out over stuffed chairs,
mussed up sheets, plumped pillows,

earrings, hair pins and perfumes
are scattered over every surface
of our Thunderbird motel room.

Cup full of womanhood we
spill over with secrets and stories
laughing long into an Elko night.

Through rain slick streets we walk
on neon, pulsing with the passion
of midnight voices drumming poetry.

You stand before the wall-size mirror:
pale skin, black lace and cat's eyes
that change color, flashing fire.

I pick up a boar bristle brush
and slide it like a song
through your sun-rich hair.

—for Kathy Ogren

Like an Ember in Hand

On a day of relentless wind,
annoyed, tired after a long
night checking heavy heifers,
I curl on the sagging couch
comforted by crackling fire,
shoulder-draped serape
and a wool afghan wrapped
round my legs and feet.

My eyes droop but I read on—
soaking your poetry like rain
into the shrivel of my dried skin,
absorbing a liquid river of lines
flowing uphill from your distant desert
to my mountains until I sleep.

The silent house wakes me.

The dying fire gives way
to slow creeping cold.

Like an ember in hand
I clutch your book
as if your words alone
could warm and save me.

—for Linda Hussa

The Writing Chair

Wicker and sheepskin, her work place
is tossed with embroidered pillows and
sunlight which streams in an open window
where checkered curtains, drawn back,
invite in the earth and dawn air.

Old photos grace the walls
new photos line the wide white sill
papers clutter the round table
where she sits intent, powerful,
lovely in her aloneness,
focused on inner reflections
of captured clouds, light, shadows.

When the words come right
they miraculously bond
like the chemical magic of epoxy glue—
a drop from one
a drop from two
stir thoroughly
and suddenly a poem sets up
stuck forever in her mind
mated with memories.

"Forget your skin," she writes,
"the trembling vein in the temple,
blue, shallow, eager...lovers
hurt more with unmet eyes
than with a back hand blow."

—for Linda Vinson

Fortune

He gave her a part of herself
she never knew existed
until he held her in his eyes
and what reflected back
was bold and beautiful
a woman no one else could see.

And so she loved him in a quiet way
worshipping the words he spoke
honoring his hands
and the way they moved
like the warm Texas wind near her face
lifting a strand of honeyed hair
from her damp cheek.

Miles and the simple measures
of separate lives distanced them
for years at a time
but she never forgot
the fortune she found
every time she heard his voice
every time he whispered her name.

—for Melinda Harvey

Old Silver

Shoulder to shoulder at the chipped kitchen sink
they stood quietly cleaning a mis-matched place setting
picked out at a pawn shop on Sixth Street: a dessert fork,
a butter knife, a teaspoon, a soup spoon and a mystery
spoon, long-handled, with a strange shaped bowl.

Polish and tarnish blackened their hands
as they shared the same soft cloth and
chatted companionably about the book festival,
the National Wildflower Research Center,
her son entering high school in August.

Hot, humid, summertime stickiness
and the boy's bold presence kept them
from touching, pressed back the kiss
that hung suspended between them
all day in the heavy, expectant air.

Leaving for home, her silver clutched tight,
she cried. He washed the sink twice,
thought of her swollen lips, dreamt that night
of an unusual shiny spoon and feeding
her tiny bites of cool raspberry ice.

—for Evelyn Green

An Image Out of Africa

With her tawny veldt of hair
she is an image out of Africa
with astounding eyes,
gazelle-wide, bright dark,
trembling on the edge of fear
and the need for flight.

Held spellbound by his smell
she is stalked so softly she is unaware
that the sound of his song in the night
is only the echo of lovers' voices
caught up in tall grass.

She whispers her secrets to me
and I give her away:
tell him all he has to do to have her
is hold the hands she's hiding,
turn them slowly over
and press ardent lips
to her damp open palms.

—for Jody Logsdon

Three Days in September

I.   Seventeen crows fly
across the pale face
of a three-quarter moon.

II.   Grey body flattened,
a coyote darts
through thick sage.

Sashaying damsels and dragons
tease trout in the shallows
of South Lake.

III.   Lunar glow dims the dog star;
elk, on the move in white moonlight,
twang top wires on pasture fences.

Snug in my sleeping bag
an old ghost licks the cold
edges of an unpalatable dream.

All night long
a she-owl's calls
go unanswered.